It's Not Going to Rain

Written by Dori Hillestad Butler

Illustrated by Obadinah Heavner

It was a warm and windy spring day.
Adam and Kelsey were flying kites.

"I think it's going to rain," said Adam. "We should reel in our kites and go home."

"It's not going to rain," said Kelsey.

"I bet it will.
Look up there,"
Adam said, pointing.

"Do you see that bear?
He's got a big bucket of water,
and he's going to pour it
over the whole town.
Then it will be raining buckets."

4

"Yes, I see the bear," said Kelsey.
"And I see the bucket,
but that bear wouldn't dare
pour water on our town."

5

"Oh yes he would," said Adam.

"Bears are sneaky.
They like to play tricks on people."

"Look over there," said Kelsey.
"Do you see that grumpy gorilla?
Gorillas don't like tricks,
and they don't like water,
and they really don't like bears.
That gorilla will scare the bear away.
It's not going to rain."

7

"Yes, it will," said Adam.
"Look over there.
Do you see that elephant?
He will toss the gorilla into the trees.
Then there will be nothing
to stop that bear
from dumping his bucket of water
on the town."

8

"I see somebody who will stop him," said Kelsey.

"Who?" asked Adam.

"Look over there."
Kelsey pointed.
"Do you see that giant?"

"Yes, but how will he stop the bear?" asked Adam.

"He will chase the elephant and the grumpy gorilla and the bear," said Kelsey.
"Then he'll drink the bucket of water. It's not going to rain."

10

"Yes, it will," said Adam.
"Look over there.
Do you see that spaceship?"

"The aliens on that spaceship
will beam the giant aboard,"
said Adam.
"So then the giant
won't chase the elephant,
and the elephant
won't toss the gorilla,
and the gorilla
won't scare away the bear.
Then there won't be anything
to stop that bear from dumping
his bucket of water on us."

12

Kelsey looked at Adam.
"An alien spaceship?
Now you've got to be kidding.
There are no such things as aliens!
If you don't want to fly kites anymore,
just say so.
We can find something else to do."

13

14

"I thought you said
it wasn't going to rain,"
said Adam.